MICRO-EXPRESSIONS: Reading Anyone's Hidden Thoughts

Dylan Clearfield

G. Stempien Publishing Company
Copyright © 2016 by Prism Thomas

Editorial offices in New Quay, Wales UK (CYMRU)

ISBN 978-0-930472-24-5

CONTENTS

GETTING STARTED

There is a way to know what a person is thinking. It isn't a trick and it isn't by magic. And it isn't through clairvoyance, although I suspect that many so-called mind readers use the method I am about to describe, possibly without even knowing that they are using it. In one sense, it may truly be a gift they possess – one which they confuse with the paranormal.

What I'm referring to is the ability to read a person's micro-expressions. A micro-expression is a fleeting – almost imperceptible facial exhibition – that is produced by a person's subconscious. It reveals what that individual is truly feeling. It is often exactly the opposite of the words being spoken which is why it emerges from the subconscious.

There are two ways to read micro-expressions: as they occur or after the fact with the use of pictures and other video. While reading micro-expressions after the fact has its uses, the most benefit is gained by reading them as they occur. It is immensely more difficult reading micro-expressions as they occur, but also immensely more beneficial as they reveal to the reader what the person who is speaking is truly feeling, despite the words they are stating.

This concise but comprehensive work is going to focus on reading micro-expressions as they occur but it will also deal with reading them from video. Most people can be successful at both methods. This doesn't mean that it's easy. But it is a skill that can be learned. And as with most other skills it is the practice of it which makes a person proficient at it.

Some people will grasp the application of reading micro-expressions quickly. For others it may take longer. Just as in playing a piano or guitar.

As an anthropologist, reading micro-expressions is a process I have been involved in for many years and have touched on the method in my earlier work, "Analyzing Anyone on Sight." In this book I am going to expand upon the skill and reveal how anyone can read and understand the hidden thoughts of others by deciphering their micro-expressions.

Images of well-known people will be used as subjects to study micro-expressions. Among the people selected for study will be: Adolf Hitler, Richard Nixon, George Clooney, Oprah Winfrey and Sarah Palin.

Why this specific group of people? One reason is because they are public figures. But as importantly, each one of these individuals revealed a deeply hidden and highly important emotional response in their micro-expressions that were examined for this book. In these responses, each in his or her way highlighted a significant facet of studying micro-expressions which establishes the validity of this field of study. By that it is meant that the hidden thoughts they were concealing were revealed and verified by the micro-expressions they were exhibiting.

These "celebrities" later acknowledged that these hidden thoughts were what truly were in their minds at the time. That is why out of the hundreds of potential sources of study and hundreds of hours of examination of videos this one small group was chosen. Their secret revelations and the acknowledgement of them afterward are incredibly rare.

Before plunging into the subject of micro-expressions, however, a person must know how to recognize a micro-expression and to know exactly what to expect when looking for them. But even before that a person must know what <u>not to look for</u> in order to not waste time seeking the wrong clues.

WHAT A MICRO-EXPRESSION IS NOT

A vital part in learning how to read micro-expressions is learning what a micro-expression is not. It saves a lot of time knowing what not to focus your attention on as already noted.

A micro-expression is not something that appears plainly on the face **and** lingers there for longer than a thousandth of a second. It is not an expression that is so striking that you can't miss it. In fact, you are not supposed to see a micro-expression by its very nature.

It's not something like this:

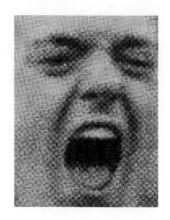

Or this:

Or this:

Why not? Because these types of expressions by their very physical nature must remain on the face for enough time to be recognized for what they are. These are fully developed expressions which in their creation take up time and space and are not subconscious images secretly appearing, then disappearing, before anyone can notice they've appeared. Micro-expressions are not meant to be consciously seen but unconsciously understood. The above expressions were made TO BE SEEN and by their very nature they must appear on the face for longer than a thousandth of a second.

In almost all cases, a person's micro-expression is not only meant to be hidden but the person making it doesn't even know she's displaying one. While she may feel the emotion that produced the micro-expression she will not be aware that she is generating an image of it on her face.

The primary point being made is that if you can easily see an expression that someone is making it is not a micro-expression. This applies to one that is being studied on video as well. Some people believe that just because an expression is of a shocking, somewhat fleeting nature, it is a micro-expression. It is important not to be lead astray by these types of emotional manifestations.

It isn't any secret how this person is feeling:

What is sought from a micro-expression is insight into the inner, hidden feelings of a person which he isn't displaying. What is he really feeling but not saying or showing? This is what a micro-expression will reveal.

And it works the same for both men, women and transgendered people. Anyone who has feelings is susceptible to allowing them to escape without warning. And this can cause a lot of trouble if the emotion being hidden is guilt or deceit.

Common facial and body language is also something that is not a primary part of a micro-expression. However, they may give clues as to what may be forthcoming from the subconscious. It is helpful to realize that when a person scratches the back of the neck or plays with the bridge of the nose or tugs on the ear that this may imply a certain amount of deceit taking place. However, it is also possible that these actions may not be related to a micro-expression that may be shortly revealed.

The point is this: if a common facial expression or type of body language is the kind that usually reveals deceit this does not mean that any subsequent micro-expression also concerns deceit. In fact, it probably won't. It may reveal just the opposite intention. Don't be fooled by the obvious expression that may precede a micro-expression.

By the way: if all of this seems very confusing – it is – don't worry because it will be reviewed many times in many various ways. And when the images of micro-expressions are studied things will become much clearer. There's a lot to learn. But it will be well worth it.

There's another important reason why ordinary facial and body language may not help when observing micro-expressions. Facial and body language can often be modes of deception. In the cases pointed out above the actions of scratching the back of the neck, playing with the bridge of the nose and ear tugging are meant to deceive the viewer. Their purpose is to hide from view parts of the body that turn color – or blush – when a person is nervous.

A micro-expression performs just the opposite function. While it reveals what the person is really thinking it is an expression not intended to be seen. As such, micro-expressions are at cross purposes with ordinary facial language. Certain forms of body and facial language are used to deceive, while micro-expressions expose the inner self. And micro-expressions also involve color change to the skin; but there isn't an attempt to hide it.

Remember, micro-expressions occur without warning and last less than a thousandth of a second. That's why if the goal is to view and decipher them the price is constant, uninterrupted vigilance. The reward will be insight that can be gained in no other way short of administering a truth serum.

Now that you know what not to look for, let's focus on what a person should look for.

MICRO-EXPRESSIONS – BASICS

As noted, a micro-expression will appear suddenly. There will not be any warning. It will be clearly visible. And it will vanish before you can even point it out to anyone else. A micro-expression will stand out like a face illuminated in a mirror by lightning. Then it will be gone.

A text book definition of what a micro-expression is will be helpful. A micro-expression is a subliminal movement which appears at any location on a person's face and reveals what she or he is truly thinking or feeling which is usually contrary to the words that he or she is speaking at that moment or a belief or feeling that this person is promoting or defending.

And remember: micro-expressions are not meant to be consciously seen but unconsciously understood.

In order to see a micro-expression you must be primed to view it. You must be as if sitting on the edge of your seat, glaring single-mindedly into the face of the person you're studying. Your sight must remain focused on her face and her face alone. Because that lightning flash can occur at any time and give that one glimpse into the subconscious of the speaker.

And it may not come at all. The person under observation may not reveal any micro-expression. She may either be so guarded and well-disciplined that her subconscious is kept entirely under control; or she may have nothing to hide or reveal. The latter is unlikely. Most people have an underlying emotion – not necessarily negative – that they are hiding. It could even be something positive, something that makes her very happy.

Most people are familiar with the "good cop" "bad cop" concept concerning the interrogation of a suspect. And most people are aware that part of the reasoning in using this technique is to obtain information from the subject by causing him to bond with the "good cop" who is trying to keep the "bad cop" under control and from using force and other unpleasant measures to force the incarcerated person to give information.

There is another aspect to this technique which few people think about and which is another of its important purposes. While one of the cops is interrogating the suspect the other cop is closely and quietly watching for any micro-expressions that might appear on the face of the person being questioned. Of course, this could be done by a third cop who is viewing the questioning from behind a two way window. At any rate, searching for a micro-expression is important in any type of interrogation. Even when made by parents, employers, nuns, or the dreaded loan underwriter.

When a person speaks he can censor his own words – often without even knowing it – and tell a story that is at odds with what really happened. His body language and facial expressions are another matter. These are generated by the subconscious. It isn't easy for anyone to fool his own subconscious. Many authorities think that it is impossible for anyone to fool his own subconscious. The truth will seep out no matter how hard a person tries to keep it suppressed.

The most important thing to remember is that while a person's words may be lies his micro-expression reveals the truth of his unguarded subconscious. As I like to phrase it: micro-expressions do not lie even if the person does.

Now this is where it gets pretty confusing. When studying for micro-expressions it is important not to overly focus on the subject's body or facial language. Sounds contradictory but it isn't. Here's why.

15

Body and facial language have to be translated based on several considerations. And their purpose is not to reveal the truth but to provide the person making these movements a way to deceive any viewers. An action like scratching the back of the neck can only be interpreted based on understanding of what it signifies rather than the act itself. Of itself, scratching the back of the neck doesn't really reveal anything.

Micro-expressions are just the opposite. They represent exactly what the person making them is feeling emotionally. Because they come directly from the subconscious they are uncensored and have a different purpose from ordinary body language; they are true feelings.

The difference between micro-expressions and ordinary body and facial language is that they are not supposed to be seen by anyone. They appear in such a rapid fashion and remain "visible" for such an incredibly short time that they are made not to be seen. And because of this protection – which the subconscious is aware of – the expression that is made is exactly what the person making it feels. There isn't any attempt made to censor it.

While on the other hand, basic body language has to be deciphered.

Micro-expressions are usually stark and usually unmistakable. They will be grimaces, bared teeth, tongues stuck out, puckered faces: they will show you exactly what the person making them feels – uncensored. Because the subconscious assumes no one will see these expressions it doesn't try to conceal or camouflage them. That's one of the major differences between basic facial language and micro-expressions.

Here's where it gets really tricky and really difficult for the interpreter of micro-expressions. The micro-expression is made in direct response to whatever specific subject the speaker is addressing. A person may be telling you how wonderful the new catheter is that she is using while at the same time her eyes deepen with the most profound sadness. She is really telling you how incredibly miserable using the catheter makes her. This is a true example that I witnessed.

The example just related is an important teaching piece for another reason, too. Before I was able to decipher the woman's hidden micro-expression I felt a sudden and powerful sadness for no apparent reason while in the midst of watching her speak. What I was sensing was a micro-expression. I felt it before realizing it existed. Thus, the experiencing of a sudden, strong emotion for no apparent reason while observing a speaker is a tip off that a micro-expression may have been displayed.

Reading a micro-expression is like proofreading a person's face. When reading a micro-expression understanding the content of the flow of words is forsaken for understanding the meaning of each important subconscious image that appears just as when proofreading a story, a person does not focus on the content of the writing but the correctness of the grammar.

Yet, using the same comparison, when studying for micro-expressions the reader must be aware of the scope of what is being said otherwise there will not be anything against which to judge the micro-expression. If someone is professing how happy she is while at the same time a micro-expression of deep sorrow flickers briefly on the face, seeing this will give an indication of what the speaker is truly feeling.

And it is the same when proofreading a story because a person must have a general concept of the subject or else nonsensical sentences might be allowed to escape detection just because they are grammatically correct.

Another example is that of the court reporter who is taking verbatim notes of what is occurring in a courtroom, one of my former professions. She is singularly focused on the individual word that is spoken and doesn't usually comprehend in depth the subject matter being discussed. Yet at the same time she must have an overall understanding of what the speaker is saying without becoming lost in the specifics. This, too, is a good example of what reading micro-expressions is like.

MICRO-EXPRESSIONS OF ADOLF HITLER

Adolf Hitler's face is certainly one of the most recognized in the world. We are going to view it now in a way that may never have been done before. The images about to be studied were taken from one of his most famous speeches. It was shortly after the burning down of the Reichstag Building – the building that housed Germany's government. Some of these images may be disturbing so please be warned.

Hitler claimed that the fire was started by Communists. Most people believe that Hitler himself was responsible for the blaze. Regardless of who started the fire, Hitler used it as a way to gain total control of the German government.

During the speech about to be examined, Hitler furiously argued that if he had been in control of the government this disaster would have been avoided. The Reichstag building would still be standing and the Communists would have been banished into nonexistence. After the speech, Hitler got what he wanted - control of Deutschland.

In order to obtain the images of Hitler about to be dissected the film of his historic speech was laboriously examined frame by frame. One thing that is immediately noticeable about the Fuhrer is that he is always agitated. Even when he isn't speaking. There seems to be a permanent expression of anger, rage and even hatred on his fate. He must have been a very miserable person.

Does this look like a happy man to you? And he's actually just standing there listening to someone speaking.

This is simply the way that Adolf Hitler naturally looked. And these images were not selected intentionally. These are random photographs of Hitler. The book can be filled with them, but you get the point.

A person wearing a perennial expression of rage and hatred is exceptionally rare. In fact, it may actually be unique. I have yet to find another person whose face is set in a constant expression of hatred. The only other person I could image who might share this trait would be Judas. Of course, there aren't any pictures of him that exist.

It's an interesting comparison, however, because in one of my other books I put forth the possibility that both Hitler and Judas were possessed by a demon sent by Satan. But this is another matter.

While the first two photographs shown of Hitler are simple still frames of him, the following picture is actually a micro-expression. It lasted for but the blink of a moment. It is the face he made just as he was beginning to address the crowd.

This is the real Hitler. This is what he really felt about the people he was about to address. But they didn't see this. Like any true micro-expression it was there and gone before anyone could consciously notice it. However, there may have been those who subliminally recognized it. It took a still frame taken from a film to capture it.

Study this expression and ask yourself what message is it giving?

Disgust? Loathing? Revulsion? To me it looks like he is sickened by the people he is about to address. Isn't this the face of someone who is about to vomit?

Remember what is known about micro-expressions. They last about a thousandth of a second and are almost invisible to the observer. They are not camouflaged. In other words, they show exactly what the person making them is really feeling. Since micro-expressions originate from the subconscious the mind does not feel the need to censor the expression. And they are usually in direct opposite to the words the person is speaking or the emotion being expressed.

But in the speech that follows Hitler is about to tell the German people how important they were to him and to the future of the Fatherland.

In this case Hitler made the micro-expression before he started speaking. Thus, his feeling of disgust and loathing was directed toward the crowd itself. But, in the speech that follows, Hitler will indeed say the words that tell the German people how important they were to him and to the future of the Fatherland.

Hitler's written records stating his true opinion of the German people was something quite different. According to him, if the war went badly and the Allies were victorious the Germans had only themselves to blame because they didn't possess the courage or inner strength for the task at hand.

These types of feelings expressed by Hitler should not be a surprise to anyone. After all, he isn't widely thought of as a benevolent, fun-loving, all-sacrificing avuncular personality. But what about his sexuality?

Why bring this up? Because it is a highly significant part of the madman's personality. He was a well-known pervert. One of his own relatives was forced to commit disgusting sexual acts with him and when she could not bear the humiliation any longer she killed herself.

It was almost impossible for Hitler to have normal sexual release. One reason was the fact that he was cursed with what is termed a micro-penis, a genuine physical disability. Very few people are aware that one of the ways he expressed sexual accomplishment was by delivering impassioned speeches. In a very real sense he became so aroused by the act that he often experienced an orgasmic type of release during the height of his ranting oratories.

Note the still frame photographs taken from one of these impassioned speeches. Are these not the final stages that a male's face assumes during the completion of an orgasm?

This next frame that is upcoming is the one people generally do not see. It is the micro-expression of the Fuhrer gaining release. I apologize for the disturbing nature of these images but they reveal what was actually taking place in the warped mind of this man while unleashing his speeches on his unsuspecting listeners, actually violating them with his words.

Does he not actually seem to be smiling in the above photograph? That is an indication that something is amiss. This is a person for whom smiling is not a normal expression. And most men will recognize the type of smile this is. Also, note the positioning of Hitler's left hand (mid-lower right of photo).

Was it not Henry Kissinger who observed that power is an aphrodisiac? In Hitler's case it literally seems to be the truth.

In one further irony, psychologists have revealed that the commission of arson is in fact usually a sexual act performed by an abnormally repressed individual. Burning down the Reichstag would have been particularly arousing for Hitler, wouldn't it?

Why examine these disturbing images of Hitler? As a warning. Perhaps in the future we would be wise to more closely examine the video of the speeches of those who plan to become leaders of a nation or even a world.

Although outside the scope of this work: consider the coming of the Antichrist who is prophesied as being a great orator. So was Hitler. How similar to Hitler will be the facial characteristics of the Antichrist when giving his world engrossing speeches. Think of it.

PSYCHOPATHS

(Some of the following is borrowed from an earlier work of mine). People who are anti-social and who have psychopathic tendencies can be identified by their facial expressions, or lack thereof. Trying to communicate with these people is both pointless and extremely dangerous. These are people devoid of consciences and suffer no remorse at inflicting pain and even death on innocent victims. Fortunately, for the trained observer – which you can become – these types of people can quickly be identified by their unique facial characterisitics.

Below is the face of a psychopath, a cold-blooded killer.

This is not an ordinary face. Can you spot the qualities that make it different from an "average" person? Most psychopaths share these features.

Note the eyes very closely. What is missing?

These eyes do not show rage. They don't show hatred. They have absolutely no emotion connected to them at all. They belong to a person who is devoid of human feeling and lacks a sense of conscience.

This is not simply the face an emotionless person. There are many people who have what are called deadpan faces and simply do not show a great deal of feeling. The face of the convicted cold-blooded murderer above goes far beyond that.

Look not only at the eyes of a psychopath but also at the lower third of the face from the bottom of the nose to the end of the chin.

There is a complete lack of animation, of any type of rigidity to this portion of the face. The word soulless comes to mind. It could belong to a storefront dummy.

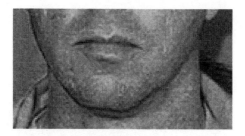

Below are the eyes of another bona-fide psychopath who committed a brutal murder.

Next is the lower portion of the face.

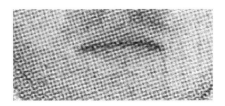

No lines, just a blank face. A face without animation. Just coincidence? Compare the first two psychopath's lower faces. See a similarity?

The eyes of a psychopathic woman show the same lack of feeling.

Not just that, there is also a drowsy type of appearance to them as if this person was simply tired of the world and everything in it.

These are not staged photos, but pictures of actual psychopaths. Below is a series of photos of the eyes of convicted mass murderers – psychopaths – so that you can see how similar these traits are.

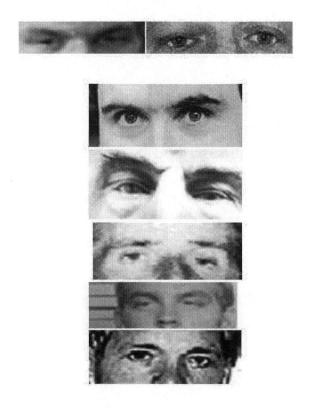

As already noted, it isn't just the eyes that give these soulless people away. Below is a series of photos of the bottom portion of their faces. Notice the singular lack of expression on all of them. Can this be mere coincidence.

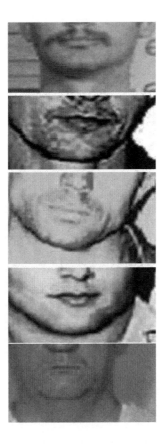

The features that are being singled out are the LACK OF emotion. Have you ever felt as if someone was "looking through you?" That should be an immediate warning. It's the opposite of that person who is jabbing you with his eyes. This is also a person to be feared, but he is more obvious. Most people are immediately made uncomfortable by a person who locks an unrelenting stare on them or whose face becomes fierce with rage. It isn't that these people are not to be feared, simply that they generally are not psychopaths.

Ironically, one of the signs that a person is romantically interested in another is if he or she fixes his gaze attentively on his object of attraction . But the feeling one gets from this should be warm and inviting not chilling and frightening. And the psychopath's gaze would be quite different.

A cold stare locked upon you is not the type of attention you should seek. And don't fool yourself and think that he will "come around" and turn out to be just a troubled person who you can help. You can't.

There are two other types of psychopathic facial features of which you should be aware. One of these is the quizzical gaze. The odd feature of the quizzical gaze is the intensity of hatred within it and the total lack of provocation initiating it. A person simply carries this look on his face as a type of weapon. Fortunately, it's an expression that cannot be mistaken for anything but pure hostility. An example follows:

Very few people would be attracted to a face like this. It is the quizzical nature of this type of face which is so puzzling. It's as if this person is questioning how there can be so many worthless people in the world and how any one of them could have the audacity to be in his presence.

There is a third type of psychotic face for which one has to be especially alert. It is the one of captivating, disarming charm.

This is a terrifying face. Why? Because the mind of a person such as this has deluded even itself into thinking that it is in truth only a fun-loving, good-hearted individual whose crimes are minor incidents. Murder to people such as these does not have much meaning.

There are two ways to identify a seemingly jovial, pleasant face such as this one as being truly psychotic. The eyes have a quality where they actually appear to be twinkling. This is totally opposite to the evil that occupies this person's mind. That's a major clue. An impossible inconsistency. Evil disguised by a veneer of pure goodness. Fortunately, there are very few people who can achieve this master deception.

The second clue follows similar lines: an impossible inconsistency. Note the eyes below:

These are the squinting eyes which unsuccessfully tried to fit a woman's forced smile. (This is just an example. She is not a psychopath.) It is physically impossible to create a genuine smile with squinted eyes.

Compare these sets of eyes:

The eyes on the left are squinting but in the midst of a genuine smile while in his mind is evil hatred. It's a feat reserved for the distorted mind of the soulless psychopath who has convinced even his own subconscious that he is a benevolent person.

However, once his true self is revealed, note how the confessed killer Joran Van der Sloot's face adopts the same features of a typical psychopath. Note the empty eyes and the non-responsive lower third of the face.

The edited photo below is extremely telling. Van der Sloot's "happy" and smiling eyes have been transposed over the eyes in his mug shot. Note how they suddenly aren't "happy" and smiling any longer but appear sinister.

Evil eyes.

Charming eyes (But the exact same set of eyes!) placed above an emotionless bottom part of the face.

This is a shocking transformation! The true evil that is within his eyes is drawn out when placed in what could be termed a neutral setting. The point is that there are certain people who can project a genuine charm which overlays the true evil within them and the most effective way of "seeing through them" is by reading micro-expressions that appear on their faces. At some point, an expression of evil may cross this person's face, which will identify the true nature of the individual in question.

In the photo below, a pair of someone else's evil eyes are highlighted and have replaced Van der Sloot's charming eyes. This is the type of signal to look for.

Rather frightening, isn't it? These are a pair of obviously psychotic eyes transposed upon the "charming" face of Van der Sloot. Remember, when a micro-expression takes place there often is a slight change of color at the location the expression occurs.

Just be warned, psychotic faces are many and sometimes clearly show a mindless detachment from reality. Below are two felons from two different time periods. The similarity is striking.

Hopefully, this section has been helpful in giving a warning about the types of faces that are common to psychotics. The similarities are not coincidences, but they are as yet not fully inexplicable. Observe very closely the face of any person you are meeting for the first time. There are usually clues to the underlying personality. Remember: if a person scares you there is probably a very good reason for you to be scared. Trust your subconscious.

MICRO-EXPRESSIONS OF RICHARD NIXON

Nixon is one of the most recognized of American public speakers and also one who has given to the world some astonishing micro-expressions. And he too had some very explicit messages for the American people which probably no one has ever seen. Until now.

The first group of pictures of Nixon were taken from his historic speech of August 8, 1974 when he announced that he was going to resign the presidency. In these photos he looks much like the Richard Nixon that we'd become used to seeing. He was well dressed, his hair was perfectly combed, and his skin tone was even somewhat rosy. In short, the Richard Nixon who appeared on television the night of August 8th looked relatively normal.

43

Well, relatively normal. When viewing the entire speech, he can be seen spending most of it peering downward with eyes shut. This is a signal he has something to hide. He does not want to look the viewer in the eyes. This, however, was very common during a Nixon speech.

His fully closed eyes should not be confused with a simple blink. His eyes remain closed for a considerable amount of time. This implies that he is trying to shut out the world, avoid what is happening. These are not micro-expressions. But they are definite facial language signals.

But then during this speech Nixon gets angry. He briefly shows the American public how he REALLY feels. Although he does so in less amount of time than it takes to wink the eye. It is a micro-expression of hostility which is caught on the following still frame.

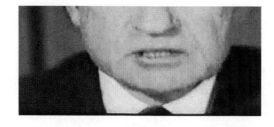

He is baring his teeth to the viewers, although probably few people actually saw it. But this is relatively mild. A few minutes later, he becomes even clearer in how he felt about the viewers.

Wouldn't you describe this as a glare of hatred? Once again, however, this isn't a micro-expression. It was a clear expression on his face for all of the viewers to see and recognize. But what follows is Nixon's ultimate display of disdain which occurred with such rapidity and lasted such a short time that it was difficult to locate even in a frame by frame search.

It is blown up to extreme size because it is so difficult to see. Look very closely at his mouth. Nixon is sticking his tongue out at the viewing public. Sticking one's tongue out is a childish behavior and it means what it implies.

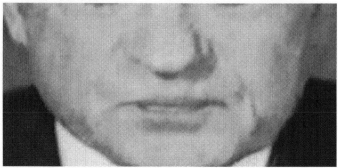

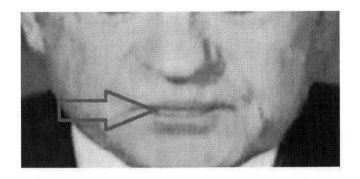

The ironic feature about this picture is that there is actually a hint of a smile/sneer on Nixon's face as he flicks his tongue out in rapid reptilian fashion. His subconscious is aware of what he's doing and it pleases him. "Take that, America!"

Is he really sticking his tongue out? Yes. There are changes in the shape of his face which are the type of changes that occur when a person sticks his tongue out rather than simply wetting his lips. It's a natural feature of facial musculature. Note the specific locations that are within the areas of black.

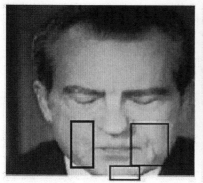

Have you also noticed that in all of the above photos the only time that Nixon's eyes are visible is during his glare of hatred? The eyes give it that full effect.

The group of photographs just examined was from the night before Nixon actually resigned. He was rather composed during this speech. But the very next day – less than 24 hours later – he had undergone a drastic change.

When the farewell speech made the next day is viewed in normal speed it is almost impossible to tell how devastated Nixon was during its presentation. But when viewed frame by frame what is revealed is the sight of a totally broken man who is constantly teetering from side to side as if about to collapse.

Particularly disturbing is the point at which he draws a folded sheet of paper out from an inner pocket.

When seen in super slow motion it is painful to watch, especially the way that Nixon seems to be struggling with his own self as to whether or not to actually remove the paper. What's on the paper? A philosophical reading about forgiveness written by a person he admired.

What follows are the images of Richard Nixon as he addresses his former staff and is about to leave the White House and relinquish the office of president to Gerald Ford. First, how he looked at the beginning of the speech.

Notice the sagging mouth and the head slumped forward as he struggles to keep his balance at the podium. He then starts his speech which in its words centers on forgiveness and not seeking revenge against those who have wronged him. But Nixon lets his true feeling out in

49

the following frame when he once again sticks his tongue out at the viewing audience.

His subconscious is in control. On his face is what he truly feels. Once again his reaction is to stick his tongue out. This photo is different from the earlier one, but note how the facial features are exactly the same. This is a micro-expression. It was uncensored because the subconscious was in control and the act of sticking the tongue out was done so rapidly that it was almost impossible to see. Such is the criteria for micro-expressions.

In case you are wondering, he isn't simply wetting his lips in this photograph. HE IS sticking out his tongue!

But there is one other clue which is exceptionally rare to capture on video. This involves the change of the color of the skin around the location where the micro-expression occurs. This discoloration almost always takes place but its duration is so fleeting that it is almost never observed. But note the photo below!

When Nixon sticks out his tongue, the color change of his skin always occurs above the upper lip. See the close up.

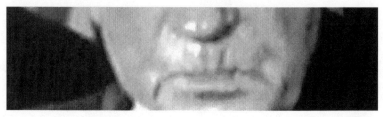

It is unmistakable. One of the truest physical signs of a micro-expression. Important to keep in mind is that while making this "gesture" with his tongue Nixon was in the midst of making a speech about how it was important not to despise your enemies but to forgive them. Hmmm?

And he continues speaking along those lines. In the midst of which he once again flashes a micro-second micro-expression to those whom he is attempting to charm.

This does not seem to be the expression of a man who is ready to forgive those who'd wronged him.

Once more his farewell speech continues to focus on the higher virtues of not destroying one's enemies because in doing so you are really destroying yourself. To this he adds one final extension of his tongue in another masterfully performed micro-expression.

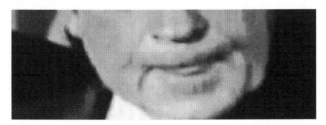

This time there's the addition of a little wrinkling beneath his lower lip.

And as in the former case of tongue extension this also is accompanied by discoloration of the skin above the upper lip.

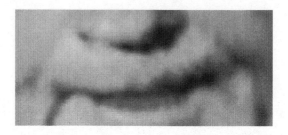

After finishing his historic speech and handing the presidency over to Gerald Ford, former President Nixon mounts the stairs of a waiting helicopter. He seems fully resigned to his fate now and is almost relieved that his ordeal is over. The characteristic wave of victory is given. But in one micro-second of time his true feelings are revealed, which in fact he tries to conceal by the wave of his hand.

A close up of his face reveals a man about to burst into tears.

He has drawn his lips tightly together in order to stave off crying and the discoloration can be seen in his chin. It was caused by the undue stress placed on that area by the pull of his lips. This micro-expression was instantly followed by the next view of him after his hand was withdrawn.

He still doesn't look too happy. But at least he fended off the tears.

You might be asking at this point: are micro-expressions this common? It seems that Mr. Nixon provided quite a few of them in a short frame of time.

Normally micro-expressions are not created in such quantity in such a short duration. However, Nixon was enduring a tremendous amount of stress during this period and would be expected to release his anxieties in any way that he could.

Also Richard Nixon was a man of deep and chaotic emotions and he was a highly secretive person. As such he would be more likely than most to reveal his true feelings in the safety of frequent micro-expressions. That is actually one reason why I chose him as an example.

DISTORTED ADVERTISING

Corporations, particularly through their advertising, use oppresive tactics to control our behavior. Body and facial language among their cheif their weapons. But the depths into the subconscious into which they reach and the methods that are used to pry into the soul is of such a brutal, invasive – yet covert nature – that it is similar to brainwashing and true mind control. The strategies used graze the subconscious in such a razer-edged way as to reflect some of the underlying features in micro-expressions on a similar, though somewhat different, level.

You already are aware of how ads are meant to overcome your objections to a product, but are you aware of how insidious the methods are? If not, you may well be so after finishing this chapter. What will be highlighted is how the distortion of reality by advertisers is one of the most powerful ways they shape the consumer's behavior. It is a warning to be ever on the alert to their methods which are a close cousin to the subliminal force wielded by micro-expressions.

If a vote were to be taken concerning who is the most disliked bully that most ordinary people are likely to meet the answer may be – a salesman of used automobiles. If he does not rank first in this area he will surely be near the top. Thus the reason that this type of ad was chosen for this chapter.

This is a composite photograph of how a car company wants you to envision yourself as a car buyer, particularly if you are female. Having access to this picture is like having a major piece of an enemy's secret code which they plan to use against you in the future.

Before I explain exactly what I'm talking about, it is important to first study the photo being referred to. It is one that has obviously been posed but which is also a composite taken from more than one source. The picture is from an ad and one purpose of the ad is to induce women to get into the mood to buy a car. The other purpose is to show her what they want her to think an "average" intelligent, analytical female car buyer would look like.

But these traits that they provide by her body and facial language are the exact opposite of what an "average" intelligent, analytical female car buyer would really look like. This is the "automobile dealer's version" of the car buyer in question.

First to be examined is the hairstyle the woman is wearing. It seems to be a hybrid of something, but I do not know what. Can you offer a suggestion?

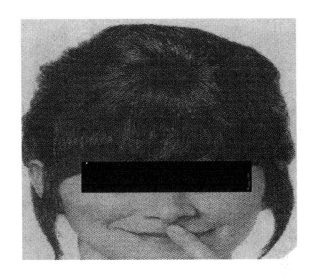

What in the name of the Flock of Seagulls (a popular band whose original members were all <u>hairdressers</u>) are those two things that are hanging down past this woman's cheeks and chin?

Flock of Seagulls

Why does she have one ear covered and the other one not?

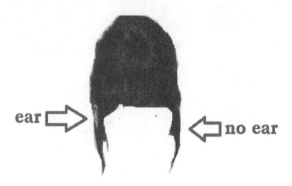

Exactly what type of bangs are those that devour her forehead?

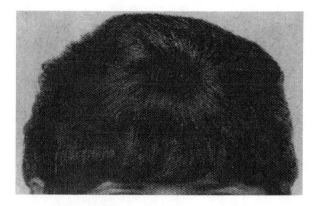

And why would any woman go out in public with a hairstyle – if it could be called that – like this? Does this denote sophistication to you?

The reason for dissecting a composite picture's hairstyle is to determine what type of impression it is supposed to have on the observer...and why? I doubt that any of you who are reading this – male or female, inbetween or undecided – have a composite hairstyle like the one above, but if you do, we will now try to determine what the message is that it is supposed to be making. Is this a message you personally would like to copy yourself?

The woman's "hair" seems to be made up of at least two wigs, one overlapping the other, supposedly representing an air of invincibility. Odd choice of words, don't you think?

In reality, they may have wanted the viewer to think: "airhead." It's a subliminal trick. You are being told that a confused, unsophisticated person is in reality an experienced car buyer and one with whom you should identify. What they are really doing through this distorted body language is appealing to your own insecurities (we all have them) and showing you that you really don't have the ability to make a reasoned decision when buying a car because YOU REALLY DON'T LOOK LIKE the supposed sophisticated person they are presenting as sophisticated.

The ad claims that this hairstyle shows an air invincibility. How does this hairstyle possibly present an air of invincibility? Maybe in the sense that anyone who would wear a hairstyle like this would have to be invincible to withstand the negative comments.

Two layers of "hair."

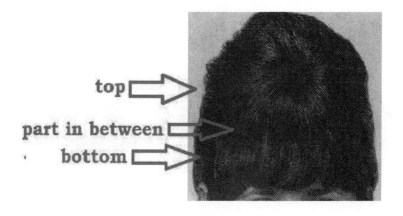

top ⇨
part in between ⇨
bottom ⇨

Continuing with the hairstyle, there is another descriptive element pointing toward one of those "sideburns?" dangling along the side of her face, referring to it as a sign of "cool determination."

It seems to be sticking out from underneath an overlying wig.

Cool determination? I cannot locate anywhere in my extensive library of body language examples where lengths of hair extending down the side of the face represent cool determination. No one looks like this. But if you don't look like this you don't possess that needed trait of cool determination, according to the ad. They are using the photo to deceive you into thinking you just don't have the "moxey" it takes to buy a car on your own.

Since this woman's hairstyle has made its point let's move on to another portion of the ad. The woman's smile is described as "savvy." Judge for yourself: savvy or not?

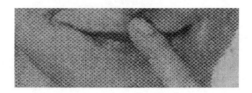

A word other than savvy comes to mind and it is a word that replaces the two v's with two p's. This type of fingertip to the lips is clearly suggestive and flirtatious.

A finger **properly** placed to the lips often does represent a person deep in thought. For example, the following photos of people with fingers to their lips show the proper poses for people deep in thought:

Keep in mind, the purpose here is not to deride these visual techniques but to explain their true meaning and then suggest their real purpose. I believe that the person who created the ad with the "savvy" female car buyer is very clever. He or she is attempting in reality to present a composite of a "typical" sophisticated female car buyer which does not look anything like any female viewing the ad. The ad is asking: you don't really look like this woman, do you? And the answer is: thus, you can't really be that sophisticated – right? Body language and its usage in ads can be quite compelling.

Next examine a very important bodily posture.

Notice how she braces her arms in front of her. This is a clear sign of blocking. It's not a sign of openness; just the opposite. Why did they place her like this? To show sales resistance. But why is she tapping her lip in a sexually provocative way and not a way that conjures deep thought? Because you WOULDN'T do that in a show room. It would be proper at a singles bar, not in a showroom because this is a flirting technique.

The whole plan is to get you to not identify with the "sophisticate" they put before you in the ad. You don't match her so you must be too gullible to really buy a car without the help of the always helpful and truthful **salesman**. That's what they hope you will think. He's the object that they are directing the reader of the ad toward.

It should be pointed out again that the pose that the woman in the ad is using is extremely attractive to a potential mate. This is because of the contradictions in her pose. She is in a pleasingly teasing posture. Her smile is alluring, her finger on her lip is actively beckoning, yet the crossed arms before her chest sends a signal to keep your distance.

This could be considered a good lesson in the art of teasing (in a sexual way). What seems like a mysterious behavior is simply a matter of mixing the proper signals – ones that attract with ones that block access. The real trick is using signals of moderate strength with none of the signals overwhelming the others. But not in a car showroom apparently.

The photo of the car buying woman that was examined was chosen for several reasons as noted. Most of them have already been mentioned. However, another important reason was for comparison. Comparison to this photograph:

Do you notice the similarities presented by the male? The pleased look with himself on the face. The folded arms across the chest. The apparent swagger. The signals being sent are almost the same but in a male form. By the way, the swagger in both the male and the female is located in the slight jutting of the hip. Imagine the two of these people meeting:

Romance in a showroom! He is the male counterpart (salesman) of the sophisticated female and will help her decide how to buy the right car.

The ad people have given a view of what a person buying a car should look like, according to them. These include many of the signals that would tell a salesperson that this might be an easy sale. Remember, a person's own chosen body language can determine the outcome of an event.

This being the case, what would be a beneficial type of body language for a person to use when confronting a car salesman? One form of positioning would be a confident stance that tells him that you aren't going to be taken for a ride (hope you appreciate the play on words).

The woman pictured above looks like she means business. Notice her slightly spread out right hand. It's basically a request for truthful information. That's a pretty confident signal, particularly when combined with her erect, direct stance. And on top of everything; the hair on her head is her own.

So, what should you do when the salesman at the dealership rushes upon you like a starving dog after a piece of steak? Keep in mind that the saleman's other weapon, aside from oppressive body language, is pressure. Time pressure. He wants you to hurry up and make your decision. A sense of urgency is used to try to force you into making a hasty choice based on his desires.

How to ward him off? Tell him you aren't ready? I like the folded arms technique.

It's difficult to argue with this stance, no matter which gender uses it.

MICRO-EXPRESSIONS OF GEORGE CLOONEY

George Clooney was a very difficult subject. I chose him for the exact opposite reason that I chose Richard Nixon. You'll understand what I mean by that shortly.

The images of Mr. Clooney that are about to be viewed were taken during a stressful time in his life. That is the time when people are expected to reveal the most amount and the most revealing micro-expressions.

He had just ended a long time relationship with one of the many female love interests. The photographs that follow were taken from a distance while he was being interviewed on the matter of his break up(s).

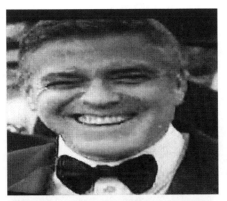

See what I mean? Nothing incriminating. And his facial language is genuine. He displays all of the features expected of a true smile. Among the most significant of these are the "smile lines" as I term them which radiate from the sides of the eyes when a person is offering a genuine and not faked smile. There weren't any micro-expressions in the above photographs.

His lack of negative reactions when asked about his personal life is just the opposite of what was discovered in Richard Nixon, which explains my earlier remark.

However, when questioned about some of his less than successful **movies**, Mr. Clooney does bristle. I will leave it up to the reader to determine what that means psychologically.

This group of photos shows him getting progressively angrier.

But none of these are micro-expressions. These are just images of Mr. Clooney being honestly angry over questions asked of him which he felt were inappropriate.

Compare them to the following image.

Tearful. He looks to be on the verge of crying. This was a micro-expression which was made instantly and wedged seemingly imperceptibly between photos of him laughing. Below is the sequence to show exactly how an apparently totally unaccounted for expression appears out of nowhere.

Most people would not have even seen the change of expression in photograph number three. They would have seen an uninterrupted sequence of laughter. And that's how micro-expressions work. They are slipped imperceptibly in between the ongoing expressions and will only be recognized by the trained observer.

Keep in mind that micro-expressions are not necessarily negative in nature. They are revelations of a true inner feeling. In the above sequence Mr. Clooney was suddenly overcome by an immense sense of sadness. What caused the sadness? Whatever was being asked at that moment is what caused it.

He was at first being asked about his various relationships, but abruptly the topic changed. The moment he broke into a sad expression was when he was questioned whether or not his relationships had had any bearing on his recently less than successful movie ventures. This is what caused the sudden change of expression.

MICRO-EXPRESSIONS OF SARAH PALIN

The images of Sarah Palin that follow were taken from the 2013 CPAC Convention. Yes, it was long ago, but she did once run for vice-president of the United States and as such will always be remembered.

Most of her talk on this occasion centered either on attacking President Obama or making highly generalized statements about how she and the people who believed in her methods will eventually create a better United States for us all.

During her often rambling talk, I was able to capture three distinct micro-expressions. However, before examining them a look at the basic image that Sarah Palin presented while speaking might be instructive. Keep in mind, I did not make up these images and I didn't "cherry pick" them to put her in a bad light. They simply are images of her overall appearance while making this speech. Maybe there was something in the drink she was gulping on.

A displeased Sarah?

A confused Sarah?

Whimsical Sarah?

Hard at thought?

Where am I Sarah?

A normal Sarah?

This last picture is a complimentary view of her which unfortunately was very rare among the images. Her expression matched her words which at this point weren't threatening or demeaning to Obama or other Democrats. Maybe if she'd compare the images and attach them to her words she might choose to follow a less confrontational path. Not only is she more visually appealing when less provocative but her words will be received by more people. However, for the time being...

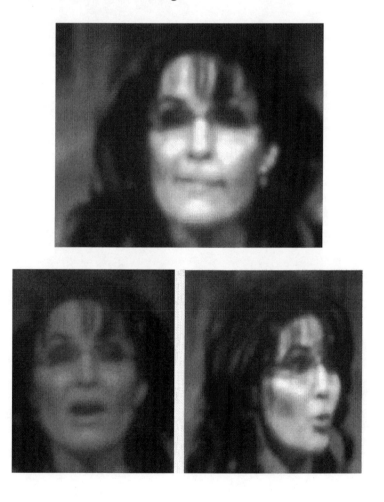

These are the common expressions made by Sarah Palin while giving a speech. The point is not to insult her but to show how the words a person chooses to use and in the way they are used determines the expression on the face. Acidic expressions accompany acidic remarks. It's a basic rule.

While none of the above are micro-expressions they are all read nonetheless by the viewer's subconscious. What effect do these expressions have on the viewer? Even someone who is a strong supporter of Ms. Palin?

Now to the micro-expressions. And they are rather striking. The first one was made while speaking specifically of Obama himself, attacking him personally. You judge.

True, deep felt animosity if not pure hatred. Gritted teeth is the sign of deep animosity. Compare this with her micro-expression when talking about one of the Obama policies she dislikes. Note the difference.

In the first instance she is verbally attacking the man's character. The person himself. In the second instance she is attacking his policies with slightly less animosity. Angry disapproval.

Next, the third Sarah Palin micro-expression. She mimicks Richard Nixon with this activity, but with a far different purpose. Note Sarah sticking out her tongue.

Her purpose wasn't to sneer at her audience but it was...it's hard to decipher. She made this quick flick of the tongue at the EXACT MOMENT when she was complaining that Obama was handing out free condoms to people. I'll let the reader determine exactly what her intention was.

Finally, we can't leave Sarah without noting one of her hallmark facial creations.

Yes, the WINK. Normally, the wink is considered one of the most sexual of facial movements. It is meant to be instantly attractive and to imply a message of readiness for...romance. However, Sarah's wink isn't the typical wink. Using the corner of her mouth, she causes the usually appealing wink to morph into more of a squint/sneer.

So, if anyone thought that this wink was an invitation to get to know her better it would be a good idea to consider something else. Her wink should be viewed more as a warning to stay away than anything else.

MISINTERPRETING SIGNS

Learning how not to misinterpret signs is as important as learning how to properly interpret them. While not concerning micro-expressions, this chapter shows how even common expressions can be seen through very different lenses. Hopefully, a little humor will be found in these next pages, too.

What is your first impression of the following images:

Problematic!

A safe place to hide?

(suggestions requested)

Santas being mugged on a ski lift?

Speaking to a non-responsive statue?

Statue trying to avoid discussion.

Police dancing down an alley?

U-turn in a literal sense.

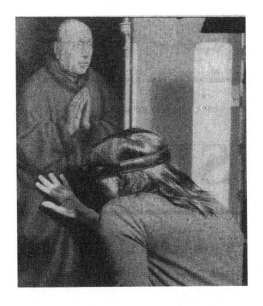

Too involved in her work?

Where IS my quarter?

Admittedly, these are not your everyday scenes and they are supposed to be humorous. But the point made is a very serious one. Signals that people are non-verbally sending are commonly misinterpreted. This can lead to a great deal of trouble, and usually unnecessary trouble. Although, I'm note sure what qualifies as necessary trouble.

You personally do not want to be fooled by one of these types of situations. Nor do you want to be the victim of giving false signals you do not intend to give.

It is very important to note how serious misunderstood signs can be. Note this next photograph and decipher what is happening in it.

First, focus on the main feature which is the man in a white tee shirt pointing toward himself with his index finger. The finger is one of the most potent of hand signals. Its purpose is very literal. It says: "Look!" "Pay attention because this is important." And it is read the same for both male and female user and observer.

Consider the signal that the pointing finger gives when you use it. It will draw attention to where you want it drawn. (This rule does not apply to cats, however. They will simply stare at your finger.) And it will almost certainly call attention to yourself as well.

But the finger point itself has many specific meanings based on the way it is used. In the photograph above, the man is pointing toward himself with his finger. This normally is a sign of confrontation. If he's pointing toward himself in a jabbing fashion the intensity of confrontation is likely to be more severe. If he's pointing directly at another person this implies a challenge. And the closer the two people are in proximity to each other the more imminent the challenge.

Consider cases when you have used your index finger to point toward yourself. What was the "point" you were trying to get across? Were you defending yourself as being the person who did much of the work around the house? Were you acknowledging yourself to be the boss. Or were you telling your co-workers to wait for your signal before clocking out early for the day?

In any event, the signal that you were transmitting was one of some degree of import. A review of the above photograph is in order.

The man pointing toward himself is black and the man observing the action is white. Has one or the other of the two misheard what he thought to be a racial slur? Is something else upsetting them? But have you also noticed that no one seems to be particularly angry? As always, a person has to interpret ALL of the available signals.

This is one of the few cases where an individual who is pointing at himself is not doing so in a way to provoke some form of challenging action. The photo was taken at a work out room at a school for the hearing impaired. The man in the white tee shirt is simply speaking in "sign" to his friend. Yet, how easily could this scene have been misinterpreted. Now on the other hand(s) we have the sight of this man below:

The two fingered jab in the air. This can't be good. If you want to double the attention, double the amount of single fingers you thrust into the air. His lower lip is slightly jutted out which is a sign that he is quite upset. But a person could probably also assume that from the angry look in his eyes.

Generally, a person who thrusts both fingers in the air like this person is a person in official authority or believes he is or should be. And, of course, our subject here is a man of official authority. He is using this gesture to emphasize his point, whatever that point might be.

It's hard to misinterpret the gist of his message which is one of opposition. There are occasions when a person may wish to have her signals misinterpreted; like a parent putting on a stronger show of authority than she might actually feel appropriate. The point would be to keep the child in line.

Concluding this section about misinterpreting signs, consider the image below. What do you think doesn't fit – seems out of place? What DEMANDS your attention in the group photograph that follows?

(used by permission)

Everybody seems so happy…except one person. I wonder why.

MICRO-EXPRESSIONS OF OPRAH WINFREY

Like many millions of people, I admire Oprah Winfrey's rise out of obscurity. She is a story of inspiration for all. Of course, it isn't by pure luck that she attained the status that she has. She also possesses something called great talent. To anyone who disagrees I suggest viewing the movie "The Color Purple."

Appropriately, the following images of Oprah have been taken from an interview she gave concerning that movie and in particular the very moment when she was informed she'd got the part in it. It was something she'd dreamt of being offered. I obtained only one true micro-expression from that interview but it is extremely revealing.

But first let's look at some of the basic facial features that Oprah displays while speaking. For Oprah – as all other people – these types of repeated expressions are what I consider to be indicators of character. While not truly micro-expressions, they do indicate a person's deeper self and, because they aren't micro-expressions, they require interpretation because they are coded.

Keep in mind, that while some of the following images may not appear particularly flattering it is their underlying meaning that is important. For example:

And:

The two things to note in the above images are the raised eyebrows and the rounded lips. These are very strong indicators and they are features that very often appear in images of Ms. Winfrey.

But what do they imply? The raised eyebrows are the sign of openness. This is common in people who are truthful, honest and open to constructive criticism. Most people would consider these highly positive traits.

Rounded lips are another common feature in images of Ms. Winfrey. Once again, this is a very positive feature. It is also very unusual for a person to possess. The rounded lips imply someone who is very caring, concerned about the welfare of others and is very generous. This feature is an excellent and natural match to raised eyebrows.

In the second image there are two other things to note.

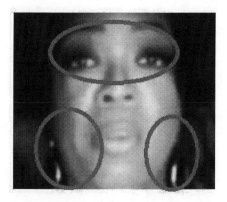

Her eyes seem sad and there are lines bracketing either side of her face. Both of these features taken together indicate that at the moment the image was taken

Ms. Winfrey was displaying concern for the well-being of someone close to her.

The next image is just for fun. What is Ms. Winfrey doing in this one?

For those of you who've ever experienced a blustery Chicago winter day when the temperature doesn't climb above 20 below zero this photo will make sense. In it, Ms. Winfrey is describing experiencing such a day and what it is like when your eyelashes freeze. Yes, this does happen.

Now the micro-expression. And it is quite revealing. The following image reveals Ms. Winfrey at the exact moment she is describing when she was told that the part in "The Color Purple" she'd wanted so badly had been offered to her.

It was a challenge interpreting this micro-expression which is one of its peculiar features. Micro-expressions are usually uncensored. But this one doesn't reveal joy or great happiness as would be expected for such an occasion. It almost looks like annoyance. When looking closely at the eyes they are on the verge of tearing. This might be a common reaction of happiness, too, as in tears of joy. But that's not the formation that the eyes themselves assumed. There is more of a sadness present.

Also, her cheeks are drawn inward in a type of displeased manner. She is troubled by something.

An answer to this micro-expression was supplied by Ms. Winfrey which adds to the validity of using this method of facial language as a way of reading a person's thoughts. She later was to say that she actually felt mixed emotions when being offered the part she had so longed for. Ms. Winfrey said she was happy but also sad at the thought of no longer having this goal to reach for. Isn't that the exact way one would describe her micro-expression?

REMINDERS

These reminders are important to remember when performing micro-expression readings and are well to keep in mind. Do not dismiss any sudden, strong, almost overpowering feelings which may strike you while observing another person. It is very likely you have just witnessed a micro-expression and that your subconscious was somewhat shocked by it.

For example, you may have felt a sense of sudden alarm when viewing this unexpected micro-expression that flashed across Sarah Palin's face during a particularly hateful reproach of Barack Obama.

Gritted teeth are a sign of extreme hostility. This expression seemed abruptly out-of-place amidst this group of images:

Or more specifically:

That is approximately how the subconscious eye would capture the sudden change of expression. But the expression would rush past so quickly that it would not be consciously visible.

On occasion, a person's normal body language may make others uncomfortable. What his body language is "saying" is also being interpreted by the subconscious but these are not like micro-expressions because they are meant by the creator of them to be understood. In this case, he wants you to feel uncomfortable. Micro-expressions are secret and are meant not to be understood by the viewer, or even to be seen.

Sticking out the tongue is a very good example. In typical facial/body language examples when a person clearly sticks out the tongue during a conversation he is sometimes stating that he'd rather not have said what he had just said and would prefer changing the subject. It is a sign that a mistake had been made.

Sticking the tongue out during the performance of a micro-expression is more often a sign of disdain by the speaker for his audience or about someone he is discussing. But this sign is not meant to be seen by anyone. In fact, the examples provided of this type of micro-expression in this book were captured with the most extreme difficulty. They were almost imperceptible. But they did occur. Note below.

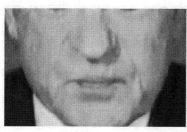

Ms. Palin seemed to even have attempted to hide the protrusion of her tongue by turning to the side. Even her own subconscious was trying to censor the action. But I observed it as did the camera. Remember, in order to produce a still photograph of a micro-expression the researcher has to believe that one has been produced and then try to locate it.

Nixon was an easier study. He frequently stuck out his tongue with disdain and it was a micro-expression to be anticipated.

Another critical feature to remember to look for at the site of a micro-expression is discoloration of the skin. It usually assumes a bluish tinge due sometimes to a sudden constriction of circulation. This occurs near the site of the micro-expression also partly because of the pressure placed on the flesh which had been forcefully stretched and then sprung back to its former condition. It is like the effect of expanding an abnormally wide yawn of the mouth. How do your lips feel afterward? They may even show some discolor along the inner edges.

Finally, when interpreting a micro-expression it is at times vital to know the deeper historical background that caused it. Sometimes the expression seems to evade any logical explanation as with the case involving Oprah Winfrey. During what should have been one of the most fulfilling moments of her life the micro-expression she revealed was sadness. Why would someone be sad when long sought success had finally been achieved?

Only Oprah herself could truly answer this. And fortunately she did so in an interview made after having produced the confusing micro-expression. She explained that she had indeed been sad at that moment because she suddenly felt a loss at no longer having that particular goal for which to strive.

This revelation of course gives much credence to the use of reading micro-expressions as a true way to reach into a person's hidden thoughts. Oprah's micro-expression had been in reality a precise impression of her feelings at that exact moment! It only had to be confirmed at a later time.

The type of secrets that can be discovered through observation of micro-expressions is unlimited. Even those that are top secret confidential.

In an impromptu interview in 2005 that was given by President George W. Bush some very highly classified information was divulged by micro-expression. The reporter asked Mr. Bush: "When are you going to release your information about the existence of aliens and unidentified flying objects?"

At this point, an expression of horror washed over the president's face, his pallor turned a zombie white, and he took a step back as if he'd been shoved by an invisible hand. All of this occurred in less than a hundredth of a second and I may have been one of the few people to have understood this reaction. On the surface, he seemed as calm and poised as ever and he continued to give a noncommittal response. But what he really revealed in his unspoken response was that he did have special knowledge about the existence of aliens and UFOs.

This is also a case where a specific question prompted the delivery of a micro-expression. What if the question had been offered in a different way? What if the reporter had asked: "Mr. President, what is your current position about releasing any information the government may have on UFOs?" It is doubtful that Mr. Bush's response would have been the same.

This implies that it is possible to draw a micro-expression from a person's subconscious if the proper question is asked in the proper format. Consider the power that this may give a person.

LASTLY

Like most talents, deciphering micro-expressions can be learned. And, like most talents, the more practice involved the more proficient a person becomes at the endeavor. The important thing to remember is to practice the correct methods. A piano player who continually misplays a piece of music doesn't learn how to play it correctly.

There are certain rules to follow when reading micro-expressions. Chief among them is constant observation of the speaker. A micro-expression can occur at any time and the observer has to be ready for when it occurs.

But there are clues to help the observer. For example, a micro-expression is most likely to occur when the subject is speaking about something of extreme importance to that person. This is the moment when that hidden – but true – emotion may reveal itself.

And, as in the George W. Bush example, if the proper question is asked it may produce a significant micro-expression.

Fortunately, the micro-expression will not be disguised. It usually will not need interpretation. That's its purpose. It is revealing the uncensored true inner feeling of the subject. It isn't censored because it is coming from the subconscious and the subconscious knows that it will be delivered within a microsecond of time and escape anyone's attention. Except for the trained observer, of course.

It is vitally important not to get distracted when seeking a micro-expression. Don't get led astray by common expressions. This is the pitfall of many beginning observers. Just because someone makes a flamboyant expression this does not make it a micro-expression. In fact, just the opposite is the norm. Micro-expressions fit neatly on the face so that they don't have to remain in view too long which would be long enough to be truly seen by anyone.

Micro-expressions are made not to be seen and not to draw attention to themselves. However, paradoxically, a micro-expression can be recognized by its clarity. It will appear for only an instant but in that instant its true nature will be unmistakable.

Also important is listening to the speaker when searching for micro-expressions. After all, you won't know what the micro-expression is a reaction to if you don't know what is being said. And this is a major difficulty in learning how to read micro-expressions. A person has to understand what is being said without paying full attention to the words. This isn't easy. The example of proofreading is a perfect analogy. You have to be able to read the words to be able to correct them but at the same time it's impossible to understand the full content of what they are saying.

This basically sums up the science of reading micro-expressions. The next step is practice. And more practice. And still more practice. It's within your reach.

THE END

Made in the USA
Columbia, SC
29 November 2020